Ordinary Fissures

§

Ordinary Fissures

Poems by

Sara Eddy

© 2024 Sara Eddy. All rights reserved.
This material may not be reproduced in any form, published,
reprinted, recorded, performed, broadcast,
rewritten or redistributed without
the explicit permission of Sara Eddy.
All such actions are strictly prohibited by law.

Cover design by Shay Culligan
Cover image by Gaston Tissandier, "Earthquake fissures,"
Illustration, Popular Scientific Recreations (Ward Lock, 1883)
Author photo by Sara Eddy

ISBN: 978-1-63980-542-6

Kelsay Books
502 South 1040 East, A-119
American Fork, Utah 84003
Kelsaybooks.com

for Benny and Hazel

Acknowledgments

Many thanks to the editors of the following magazines for publishing the pieces listed below, sometimes in earlier forms:

2River View: "Coming Back," "What Binds You"
Abandoned Mine Quarterly: "Glaucous"
Baltimore Review: "Starvation"
Causeway Lit: "Peach Jam"
Dandelion Review: "Hair," "Heron Pond"
The Ekphrastic Review: "Summer Fling"
Fine Print: "Fledgling"
Forage: "Revolution"
Glint: "Identifiers"
Gyroscope Review: "Honeycake," "Katherine"
Juked: "Lentils"
LEON: "Heavier," "Goldilocks"
Long Exposure Magazine: "Mercury Fountain"
The Mantle Review: "At the DeCordova Museum," "Pumice Mines"
Museum of Americana: "An America"
New Note Poetry: "Close"
Panoply: "Water Sports"
Pink Panther: "Naucrate"
Poetica Review: "Skinnydipping," "In a Valley"
Raleigh Review: "Buffalo Jump"
Rune Bear: "Insect Mind"
Sky Island: "Spider"
South85: "Pandemic Baking"
Spank the Carp: "55-Inch Screen"
SWWIM: "Lake Erie Guest House"
Threepenny Review: "Household Gods"
Tishman Review: "Furious"
Zingara: "Teeth"

Poems previously published in *Tell the Bees: Poems about Bees & Beekeeping:* "Furious," "Starvation," "Driving Home"

Poems previously published in *Full Mouth: Poems about Food:* "Ample," "La Voile," "Ghost," "Prep Work," "Peach Jam," "Honeycake," "Caviar," "Oysters"

Poems previously published in *Wayfinding: Poetry Celebrating America's Parks and Public Lands* (Anthology): "Yosemite"

§

For their support, love, and humor, I thank my mother, Nancy Eddy, and my children Benny and Hazel Kleinman-Eddy.

For the gifts of quiet space, respect, and beauty, I thank V. and Alice Hansmann and the Prospect Street Writers' House. For their keen editors' eyes, I thank Allison Blevins and Naila Moreira.

Numerous friends provided audience and inspiration throughout, including Julio Alves, Sam Camera, Susie Chang, Sarah James, Chris Jonas, Leilah Jones, Naila Moreira, Stephen Porter, and Rebecca Stimpson. I feel endless gratitude for the community that supports my work.

Contents

I.

The Sow	15
Furious	16
Fledgling	18
Stray	19
Flight	20
Close	21
Buffalo Jump	22
Goldilocks	23
Water Sports	24
Teeth	25
Ample	26
Yosemite	28
Laguna Beach Fossil	29
Heron Pond	30
Nauset Beach, Night	31
After the Barn Dance	32
Love Poem	33
Insect Mind	34
Starvation	35

II.

La Voile	39
Ghost	40
Prep Work	41
My Mother With Fireflies	42
Naucrate	43
In the Bed, Bath, & Beyond	44
Staging	45

What Binds You	46
Peach Jam	47
Household Gods	48
Honeycake	49
Lentils	50
Caviar	51
Katherine	52
Oysters	53
Mercury Fountain	54
Identifiers	55
Driving Home	56

III.

Ordinary Fissures	59
Glaucous	60
Storm	61
Trash Night	62
Coming Back	63
An America	64
Hair	65
55-Inch Screen	66
In a Valley	67
Fly	68
Being Alive Feels Good Again Sometimes	69
I Saw Something in the Mirror	70
Skinny-Dipping	71
Summer Fling	72
Pandemic Baking	73
Spider	74
Pumice Mines	75

I.

The Sow

We walked the mile over one day
to see the farmer's new piglets.
We didn't know they were taking them
away from the sow that day.
My hand was sweaty in my mother's grip.
A baby myself, I didn't understand
what husbandry necessitates. The spectacle of it.

The farmer's blond sons mud-slipped
in the paddock, snatching piglets
by their trotters, dangling them midair,
slapped infants. On the other side
the sow was grotesque, compelled
by rage darker than thunderstorms, witches.
She wrecked herself against fence,
battered, battered the boards until

a final feral scrambling thrust—
birth of a planet—
and she arrived,
bloody-snouted, shrieking.
She was perfect and righteous,
and my love for her was awful
when her hooves met the back
of a handsome boy, planting him in the muck.

Then everything was slick and red,
and as her tusks played ecstatic,
the piglets danced around her with joy.

Furious

A queen went mad, that summer
I was sick, lying on the green couch
day after day while chemicals
fought in my bloodstream,
and my hair came out in curly clumps
on the worn velvet.

It started subtly. Early in summer
when I was still able to trudge
out to the hives, her workers
stung me twice through my thick white suit.
Warning shots.

Then I lost track of the world,
and she gathered up
the pollen dust of my will
and spread it through her hive.
Her brood turned honey into anger.
They chased my neighbors down the road,
punished my confederate keepers.
They were pissed,
done with people poking at them.

In late summer, my blood felt deep.
I put on two pairs of pants, three shirts,
giant mudboots, thick beekeeping suit.
I cracked the hive,
and bees bubbled out in fury
banging against my helmet.
I talked to them. I told them
it would be ok, they would flourish,
pollen would be plentiful,
nectar would flow like wine.

The long dark queen beetled
across the frames. With gloved fingers
I pinched out her angry life.
I gave the hive a new queen, nestled
between the frames in a little wooden box,
plugged up with sugar.
Within weeks they settled.
But I felt the loss of that bitchy queen
who made her whole world a place of defiance.

The honey that fall was deep and spicy,
too complicated for tea.
I ate it on toast in small bites,
savoring her sweet resentment.

Fledgling

The morning we moved in together,
25 years ago, do you remember?
You forget these things.
We walked under the trellis
to our new front door,
and a crow crouched
on the front steps, trapping us
with one black eye, feet splayed.
When we got close, she spread wings
and clattered her beak,
snapping, staying.
A more superstitious person
would have thought twice
about her whole life.
I should have walked away, left you
and all our stuff in a truck on the curb.
I should have spent my days searching
for the meaning of that moment.
Instead we went for coffee,
and the stoop was empty
when we came back. So
we moved in, began work
on all those years.
But you don't remember this.
On the day I did leave you, decades later,
I stood under our willow tree.
In its branches a murder of crows
screamed insults at me
for waiting this long,
telling me what I had lost,
what dark potential I should have nourished.

Stray

Soft hands stroke his ears, now. Meals appear,
and love, a leash holding him back.
We were looking for magic to tame us,

give us furry comfort. We hoped for a creature
to set calm against our 21st-century terror,
a model of peace under restraint.

But he chews up books, papers, furniture,
windowsills, the ground itself. We do research.
He is just anxious, smart, half-feral, stray.

Down South he contended with bigger dogs,
and slept on dusty red plains.
He didn't know houses or a name.

He shows us with his eyes that people
might kick you as soon as feed you.
Trust is a rumor passed on by the pure-bred.

But all his magic is unbroken. He urges us to run
nimble through woods, face hard truth
with wily strength, and put our teeth to fear.

Flight

My son is a California Condor,
wingspan stretched out to 6 feet,
lanky long legs, hair tousled
in a cowlick crest. He's a giant
bird that nestles in a small space,
his wings hugged around him.

He takes the world hard,
but does not complain, finds
no purchase in grievance.
The room is tight with angles,
a tent triangle with 3 feet of ceiling
in the center, a runway,
the only place he can stand full up.

His aqua blue room holds
him close under the eaves.
Rain patters on the roof
of our old yellow house,
mice scurry in the walls
and the sleeping is good.

But soon the world will be eddies and wind currents,
and he'll batter his wings on the walls.

Close

I'd like to watch a film
about a little girl like me,
and her unlikely friendship
with some large animal—
a grizzly bear, say.
It eats at me, a craving.
I can see the edges of the plot:
they save each other,
she buries her face in his fur.
In the end, she surrenders
gratefully when he puts
his muzzle to her throat.

Buffalo Jump

A cliff juts out, edge fragile,
crumbling under the weight
of a buffalo herd. They charge
pell-mell over the precipice, push,
jostle, fight with dank animal panic.
The ground below is out of frame;
they will never stop falling.

The artist chose to center one animal
mid-fall, in this instructive
children's-book illustration.
Its eye meets ours, rolling wildly.
I was not meant for this.

As a child, I always turned to this page first,
my belly plunging already in the panic
of unbelonging, rushing me to the edge,
my rough fur skin rubbed raw.

Goldilocks

I always wanted Goldilocks and Baby Bear
to be the best of friends, for BB to find her
in his bed and see the essential good in her.
I wanted Goldilocks to live cozy in the bear's house.
Papa Bear would build another bed for her, Mama
Bear would make more porridge. Because look at me,

baby me with curly blond locks, big blue eyes.
The world always took care of me, owed me
a bear friend and all the porridge, it always saw
my best intentions, my deepest needs.
Even when I broke into their house,
ate their food, smashed their furniture.

Even then, they did not call the police,
who did not arrive to suspect me of a terrible history
of crimes, who did not accuse me on the basis of my skin,
who did not shoot me dead in the living room
of my friend Baby Bear's house,
in front of his loving Mama and Papa.

Water Sports

We're under water.
We play that game
where we hold each other's shoulders
and you scream a sentence at me.
I try to guess what you say,
but it's no good.
Your voice echoes,
dulled by the water.
Ripples distort your lips,
and your lip gloss is caking.
I'm like the last child
in a game of phone tag.

Finally we crash to the surface
gasping and giggling
and I'm meant to repeat
back what you said.
I make something up,
not even a guess—an invention
to impress you, make you laugh.
I'm preposterous and clever.
And it works: you smile at me,
and we throw our bodies backward
taking the Nestea plunge.

But I know really I've failed—
I know that now we can't be friends,
and next week you'll be under water
with some other stupid girl
holding each other down.

Teeth

The neighbors' child wanders
into my yard unannounced
to play on the old swing set.
I know her mama will be along,
but I go out with a sigh
to make sure she doesn't break her head.
I say hello, but she doesn't answer.
She's full of beans
and evil intent—Loki's best girl
needs watching.

She sucks her lips into her mouth
around her teeth, preparing
for something, sparking
her eyes at me like she's ready
to leap at my throat.
She pulls her lips back
and holds them gaping,
exposing her true purpose:
a loose tooth.
She puts her tongue against it
and pops it out, letting it dangle
from a dead mouse tail. Nausea.

I leave her then to her trickster
god's care, scurry to the house,
nurse my curious distress.
Why are teeth so upsetting when
they aren't in our mouths?
Fallen out, punched, pulled, rotted,
the roots of nerve and blood go back ages
to when this would be a death sentence
leveled by a cruel god:
you lose your teeth,
you cannot eat, you die.

Ample

I've decided to move past
my salad days, my small-
pot-of-yoghurt days,
give my appetite free reign,
and crown myself
Queen of the Gluttons.

Today I will eat 3 bowls.
I'll take an extra plateful,
eat a field of greens, a pasture
of cows, a coop of chickens. I'll tip
back a crock of kimchi, gargle
it down with a flagon of rye.

I'll eat an ocean of shrimp;
I'll eat an ocean.
I'll eat the trees on Monadnock
and the mountain itself—
my mouth will unhinge
to take in, with their joy,
all the people in this town
their dogs and babies,
their sorrow, their suffering.
I'll eat their sins and the bodies
they're ashamed of,
scrape their hair from my teeth
and pull roads through my bite
like the leaf of an artichoke.

I'll roll through town with
a sumptuous belly, picking
my teeth with a steeple,
drinking satisfaction as a digestíf.

My body will be capacious
rolls of fat, a landscape of desire,
pillowy thighs of pride.
I'll take up room, I'll eat up time,
and if you call me fat,
my physique grotesque,
I will devour your judgment,
and your soft eyes will pop
like caviar between my pearly whites.

Yosemite

I was 21.
I took the bus
south from Seattle,
the Green Tortoise Bus,
seats removed
for one big mattress
where latter-day hippies
played guitar.

I was 21, and sad.
I took it south
to Joni's California.
From San Francisco,
I went east to Yosemite.

I was 21 and ancient,
I was 21 and undone until I crawled
into the belly of a fallen sequoia,
felt the soft quiet
earthly dust beneath
my hands and knees,
and began the rest of my life.

Laguna Beach Fossil

We walked up into the dry
blond hills above your house,
Baba Yaga perched on stilts
driven into the slope.
We were time-lost,
perilously close to falling
in love, but set against it.
We didn't know the path
we traced would one day burn,
flames rushing down the hills
to the Pacific, taking the stilt house
and all our letters.
But I found in the dirt that day
a monument to endurance—
a fossil scallop, two halves
with their ribs not quite meeting,
stone-cast. A thing not itself,
but its immutable shadow.

Heron Pond

Why shouldn't I stand like the blue heron,
intent at the edge of the pond
my toes deep in the muck,
my eyes meant for one thing?

Why shouldn't the swallows describe
a new geometry in my periphery
while they dive and dance
for scuttling surface bugs?

And why not feel in my bones
the gentle clatter of turtles
knocking into each other
as they play or fight or flirt—
who knows their inscrutable intents?

Why not focus my brain
down to one sliver of meaning
and stretch forward toward that meaning,
my long neck extended
my body bent forward, then
my whole self whiplashing at that goal?

The fish in my throat
would be like silver, like truth,
like an answer.

Nauset Beach, Night

The parking lot is still warm
to our feet, but the cars
have gone back to rentals
where sandy tired people
eat cold pizza and beer and nurse
their sunburns with aloe.
We've been waiting for this.
We ache for the sand
and the moon dares us
to run from dune-top to
sea-swell, surrender
to the black whole water.

But at the top of the path
by the benches and garbage
they wait for us, their faces turned
to stare like rude children,
animal hands holding prizes.
Their eyes shine behind masks.
We calculate welcome
versus threat.

The beach is a test.
For the reward of our bodies lifted
weightless on the waves, we
suffer gritty crotches and
burned feet, sand in the chips,
bruising rocks at tide's edge.
These villains accusing us.
The night wants a piece of our
human uncertainty, our
almost-fear, and it pays us
with this trash and darkness.

After the Barn Dance

It was Halloween, and we dressed as other people,
people not like us. I smeared make-up on my lips and eyes,
I performed allure and reveal, and felt uncomfortable.
You wore a suit and tie, a formal man, a stiff, difficult man.
Maybe a wedge of truth hid in our pockets.

In the barn I danced joy with all our friends,
singing Billy Bragg and Bruce Springsteen
with the pick-up band. Voices gathered
up in the rafters like barn swallows.

You stood on the outskirts, watching me with a beer
and love. But afterwards, when we stumbled through
the black woods to an icy cabin, and found our little bunks,
you left me for your own snoring comfort while I shivered.

How could I have missed it? I got up the next morning
to wander into the forest with you, to conceive our first child
on a rough blanket while hunters shot deer around us.
I rushed headlong into the frigid woods of adulthood with you.

All the clues lined up and I danced right through them,
singing patience and embarrassment till it all ran out.

Love Poem

You arrive unannounced in your little red car,
the one you drove in the '80s, resurrected here.

You pull into my driveway & getting no answer at the door,
wander down to the garden, find me working.

Brow-dirty, sweaty, I'm fully in myself,
happy, finally. Without speaking

you take me in your arms, kiss me sweetly.
I pull from my grandmother's gardening apron

the weeding knife—the one she used for excising
taproots, unwanted weeds, things invasive.

Slowly, kindly, I slide it into your soft
man's belly and say goodbye.

Insect Mind

Eyes of jade, minds of steel,
insects will rule the world soon,
when we have all burned
or drowned, and more power to them.
Let them scurry and strive.
Let them make aspirational
goals, think outside the box.

For now all I ask, stink bug,
mantis, earwig, silverfish,
is that you keep your own
unimaginable world
to yourselves. Do not crawl
into cozy dark warmth
behind my tragus-triangle
to lay your eggs at night.
Do not let your babies
speak to my brainstem
and commit me to a mind
of leafstem, greenblood, viscera.

Hold off, hold off—the world
will be yours soon enough.

Starvation

Early April and dirty snow,
tender shoots snap beneath my boots.
I hike out to the hives to listen
for the hum of life.
But when I press
my ear to the cold wood
I feel my dread crack open.

Down in the dark
between the frames
the colony has frozen.
Lifeless in a ball, their corpses
point to the center, the omphalos
that was their queen.
Their numbers weren't enough.
Their little bodies couldn't
keep her warm, and they starved
vibrating with life till the end,
a bee's length from honey.
Like the horses in Pompeii,
preserved in the traces
of harness and cart, lifelike
they labor even in death.

In the still-icy garden, I hold up
this frame of ruin, I feel my belly
drop out, the loss expanding outward—
monumental circles of decimation
and extinction, slow emergency
ripples from this gentle decease.
Hive upon hive lost, den and nest,
hole and warren, eyrie, byre
all empty, all still. I struggle
to pull myself back to just this,
just this one hive
and what I can do.

II.

La Voile

—for Stephen F. Porter

And suddenly I'm crying openly
in a French Restaurant on Newbury Street
while the waiter delivers scallops and duck.
The diners around us try not to look,
and look anyway. They think
perhaps we've split, or someone has died.

I'm old enough not to care what they think,
but young enough to feel afraid
that no amount of Magret a la d'Artagnan
or Coquilles St. Jacques will calm me down.

We're in dark waters, a lost friend, a betrayal
and my chest hurts. I'm foundering,
my friend, and you don't know
how to pull me back in.

But at last you find the right thing to say,
and I begin to breathe in the solid lasting
glow of this place and of you.
I can feel it all transforming
already, becoming memory.

What power we have, to decide what is past,
what is present, to take control
of our mind's eye, to tack or jibe,
grip time by the boom and face the wind
or give it our backs.

The restaurant is called *La Voile,*
and I'm learning to sail.

Ghost

Every week or two she pulls back
the coverlet in the unused bedroom.
That's all, or, that's all I know.
She may also be wandering
in the air and water, standing
against the walls, inhabiting my head,
filling my body with her own.
Her shoulders and biceps in mine,
her fingers in my fingers like gloves
kneading this bread. Does she leave me
and enter the dough, waking up
with the yeast to new life?
Does she drive to work, shovel the snow,
pick up the kids? She's tired out
from these days in me;
she feels in her dead bones
the ache of menopause and life.
Even the dead need to rest.
I never used to believe
in ghosts, except when I did.
Now this one lives with me,
shows me who she is,
and I don't care, I'm not afraid.
The only ghost I want is my father,
but he's floating
on some Bartok quartet
in my mother's ear.
So when I lie down in the guest bedroom
late at night, feeling her body in mine
an alien and young new thing,
I know there are scarier things than this.

Prep Work

My mother was cleaning shrimp.
It must have been a special occasion—
we had no money, and shrimp were dear.
But no, I'm wrong, she was paring an apple,
the knife curving the sphere.

No, it was definitely shrimp,
a sharp knife defining belly and back,
her perfect fingernails peeling off
the protective armor,
the lovely feathery tails.

She was wearing her green wool cardigan.
Or maybe it was summer, she was in pink
pedal-pushers, her hair reddish-brown,
or maybe it was grey, no—white?
The kitchen, 1960s chic and rooster canisters.
The kitchen, remodeled 1980s cherry,
faux-brick linoleum. But yes,

yes, I remember her hand slipped,
her knife missed its mark,
yes, it followed the curve of muscle
and momentum and then: blood
everywhere, the knife falling,
her good hand grabbing
a towel, wrapping it already red
and bleeding through, and yes
she yelled for my father,
but stayed calm, making
sure that though I was little and scared
I remember her in control,
I remember that blood requires grace.

My Mother With Fireflies

—after André Breton;
  found language from Rabindranath Tagore

My mother with fireflies
  flowers like a drowsy moth
  her dance says farewell.

My mother with golden leaves
  slumbers on waves
  and her kiss is a pond in debt.

My mother with emptiness
  dances in shadows
  and glows with fruitful burdens.

My mother with azalea strength
  makes unfathomed harmony,
  her muscles flame and play.

My mother with oleanders
  digs a soil doll's house
  in an immortal storm of secrets.

My mother with "the orb of my life"
  holds us with strong arms and breezes,
  sheds all her petals and finds the fruit.

Naucrate

What was it like for Naucrate, mother of Icarus?
Some stories cast her as "mistress" to Minos,
as if she were pampered and adored, lover

to the king, not a dark slave repeatedly raped.
Minos gave her as a gift to Daedalus—to pay for a labyrinth
no one would use as a metaphor for slavery.

When she gave birth did she labor in pain for hours, her body
torn open? Was she allowed to love her son,
to let him hold her fingers as he took his first steps?

No myth tells that story. Naucrate dropped out
of Apollodorus and Ovid and all the centuries
of myth, disappearing beneath an ocean

of indifference. She felt no surprise
that Daedalus made only two pairs of wings.

In the Bed, Bath, & Beyond

Alone for a moment, stealing
sovereignty in Bedding,
my little boy strips down
naked, pulls pillows and blankets
off shelves, and nests
himself down like an animal.

I rush back, scoop up
his smooth perfect body.
I am rational, adult,
but feel also the sharp sternum
tug of warmth, grace,
bare skin. I turn away,
stifle that sensual shaggy urge.

Instead, I pretend for myself
and the amused clerks.
I play that I'm not furious
at the bonds on my baby,
not fighting to restrain a clever
feral animal in my own chest
who longs to defend her baby's nest
with fox-tooth and blood, chaos and rage.

Staging

While you work and the children play at daycare
I suffer the last days staging the house,
teaching it to sing for strangers.

I paint the doors a bright deep blue that says
we are all happy here. I take a fairy brush and a pot
of vivid white paint and touch all the dark spots,

the dings and faults, until the baseboards are blameless.
I spend days wrestling heavy mistakes to the curb,
emptying the house because an empty house looks joyful.

Finally on the last day I trudge to the dank basement.
I have discovered the closet that is the cat's
secret place for shit and piss.

On my knees I scoop up desiccated waste
with my raw fingers, a slurry mixed with concrete silt
and disappointment, and with the will of my body

I make it nice again for the next happy family.

What Binds You

to the earth
tracked in by the dog?
How far will you go
in your attachment
to the base good
of soil, humus, loam
when the next steps are mop,
oil soap, dog bath?
Some things are good
only in the right context.
Weeds heal bee-sting
(common plantain),
encourage digestion
(yellow dock),
and make a good salad better
(stinging nettle).
But a nettle is a nettle, too.
On bright afternoons
in the currant patch your hand
brushes those leaves,
hidden among the berries.
The sting lasts for days.
You must decide:
uproot the patch, or suffer
for the sharp green tang on your tongue?

Peach Jam

Sometimes after all the work,
after cutting the cling from the stone
and excising the bruises,
after measuring the pectin
and balancing the brute
lemon with a mountain of sugar—
sometimes still something goes bad.

The pectin fails,
the peaches turn brown,
or in the final moment
a jar cracks in the boil
and the sweet peaches
swirl out with broken glass
into the canning water.

The peach jam was always
yours; I did the raspberries
with their bright tiny pips
and dilly beans pickled
with garlic and cayenne
and frustration.

I wish I could have seen
that the swirl of sweetness
and danger, yellow flash
and sticky waste—these have
their own beauty, their own
polyphony, even if in the end
we pick out the glass,
scrub out the pot,
and start over.

Household Gods

They say they are all one,
these gods I fight with.
But I see them only
as so many ghosts
sneaking around my house.

I'm the most passive-aggressive
of congregants, praying
to my goddess of bread,
asking her to plump the dough,
paying her obeisance
in sugar and flour,
water the temperature
of the blue veins in my wrist.
But to be safe I lay out cash
for high-end catalog yeast.
If the bread stays flat
the blame is with me.

I have all my own
household gods,
of computer failure,
car repair, video game win,
hair products and trip-on-the-stairs.
Chthonic gods of carrot and beet,
ethereal gods of roof shingle
and lost umbrella.

It's a light game I play.
I pretend to buck responsibility
for a minute, before rushing in
to get it all done.
Even if they are all one,
they have let down
the team, and I've been
called in, a ringer who
fixes what's broken.

Honeycake

My Son, my beautiful boy, how are you this brave
that when every part of you aches to blockade the door

and crawl into a corner, instead you say *what*
when I knock. I celebrate you, I honor your strength

the wisdom that made you tell me when your mind
had gone dark, you were straying, you needed me.

I'm throwing a party with bright balloons for the open heart
that explains to your friends that sometimes

you just can't go out, talk on the phone,
get out of bed. I'll bake a cake for you tonight

drip sugary glaze across its bundty mountain shoulders.
I'll bring a piece to your door, and I know you

won't be able to get out of bed, I know you won't
even meet my eye, but I will be prouder than any mother

of a star athlete or an honor roll king when you say
thank you, Mama and take a mouthful of honeycake.

Lentils

Soup simmers on the stove becoming soup,
instead of just lentils ham onions celery bay.
I've overheard you fighting,

you and your sweet shy girlfriend behind closed doors.
I don't know what will come of it,
whether this is the end of a year

of young silly stupid beautiful love,
or maybe just a rearrangement of ingredients.
I remember a night when I was 18, my father

picking me up from a boy's house. I was sobbing
and it was the end of the world,
and that isn't even untrue, that night

a whole world came to an end.
I was snotting and embarrassed
for my father who didn't know

about the end of the world or how girls
cry from their bellies. I hope I remember this,
I hope I remember about the end of the world,

I hope this soup helps even just a little
to make you hurt less and settle your mind
into sleep tonight. Is it different,

between mothers and sons? Did I make a mistake
in not raising you like a wolf? I gave you cakes to bake
and acoustic instruments, philosophy and fear.

Maybe that's all a parent can do—make soup
and pay attention to the stock and the herbs.
That's what my father was doing,
driving me home, looking terrified.

Caviar

—for cwh

While packing up to leave my house and marriage,
I find a tin of caviar, fish playing in a faded green sea
among Cyrillic letters on the label.

It was a gift from a boyfriend decades ago
when I was barely a woman, new in my body and luscious
with love. He had been to Russia,

and swam with thoughts of me when he saw these fish,
emblems between us of love and play.
When I packed up from that love,

tucked our letters and eternal ephemera in a cardboard box,
I added this tin, and swore I would only open it
and put my lips to those salty eggs when I fell in love again—

the young woman's prescience, that of course
I would do that, I would replace that early training-wheel love
with something more solidly, austerely adult.

And I have. I've had a whole lifetime since then
of late-night open hearts, mad sex in pine woods,
moon-gazing woozy-headed love. I had a marriage

worth at least fifteen of its twenty years,
and a love affair worth all the time it took.
They were all exquisite, all wonderful, loveable men.

But here in this box is this tin and its funny happy fish,
all these decades later, still sealed shut.

Katherine

For years we fell
into ponds, told our stories
and dressed each other up.
You had cataclysmic orange hair
and smooth ruddy deer-legs
I admired painfully.
But then we had a falling out,
and we never climbed
up or back. Does that make
the days spent skinny-dipping
and thunderstorm-dancing—
days that fill me up even now,
even 30 years later—
does that make them null,
the stubby ends
of mowed-off weeds?
The internet tells me
you're married now,
you have children,
like me you love them.
Your hair is long
and still ravishing.
I don't know your mind
anymore, though I was sure
we were linked, tethered for life.
Ours felt like a friendship
that would curl around us,
a permanent tattoo vine.
But I've spent a lifetime
figuring out how to have friends
and still I don't know how to keep them.
I explode with them,
burn them alive,
then tell myself
not to look back.

Oysters

I'm sitting solo in a bar
watching the game over
a stout and a salad
and I'm thinking of oysters.
Not of ordering them.
They make me retch, now.
But of the first time, when
you and I struggled through
snow to a cold Cape Cod bar.
We were still in love, but already
I was thinking of other seas,
salty and wild. Still,

when the waitress brought
the pearly circle, the lemon
and cocktail sauce points of light
in the midwinter grey, and
showed me what to do
(lemon-oyster-sauce, slide
the muscle body down—
how repellant, what guts
it takes, that first time),
I was focused for a moment,
in it with you, ready for anything.

And so, happy, to sit across
from you and give this my mouth.
The oyster like another tongue
spoke to mine of the ocean itself.
My head swam, my nerves stood
on edge, and everything in that small bar
watched with me to see
what I would do in
that ocean, on that day.

Mercury Fountain

I saw it then with passion eyes,
in the Miró Museum North of Barcelona,
back when we were still paying attention.
We marveled at the sinews of that silvery ribbon
Snaking through its track; childhood fevers
transformed by erotic spellcasting.
I did not really understand it,
or maybe I understood it only as I could then,
a young woman new to marriage and life.
Now we have finished our marriage,
cast aside that thrilling beauty, and I am grown.
But I feel my new self charged
with poisonous glory, cataract and splash sealed
behind glass to protect the unprepared.
I would step into that room, now
feel the mercury thread drop
down my throat to my deepest belly.
This beautiful anger makes me dangerous.

Identifiers

Deep in mossy woods,
mushrooms cluster
at the feet of trees,
quiet temptations.
I could gently
pry one back, inspect
the annulus, where
in slow-motion violence
the cap outgrew the stalk.
Look at the gills,
searching for evidence
of worms within.
Gauge the subtle
consistent color
of the honey brown cap,
gentle stubble of tiny
black hairs, like your
face when we first met,
too young to make
a man's beard.
In the end, I walk
out of the woods
with a bandanna full
of fungus, and lay the caps
out on black paper.
I look for dusty traces
to confirm these are Honeys—
not Deadly Galerina.
They are safe, trustworthy.
Is this what it takes
to forgive?

Driving Home

They're safely boxed, I promise,
swaddled in mosquito netting besides.
The hive sits solid on the back seat,
but I'm driving gingerly,
as if my firstborn
were cradled in a car seat.
I can hear them humming, not angry
but ready, for what comes next.
The box warms with their friction.
It feels as if their potential energy
is powering the car, my life.
The next few months
of my failing marriage.
I'm holding the wheel gently,
keeping to the speed limit.
I've got 20,000 bees, and new hope,
and I feel weaponized.

III.

Ordinary Fissures

A tree falls in the back yard, exposing dark
caverns beneath. The dog is hit by a car; changes

in its personality appear. It's fall, the leaves
fall. A door swings shut. You find a fossil

far inland, where it's been desert for millennia.
There's a patch in a wall—a window,

but now it's bricked up. Your father, it turns out,
is not your father. The cancer comes back.

On the street a stranger smiles as if they know you.
A young child holds clear memories of a past adulthood.

The cat, smelling death, curls up beside the dying.
Plans change and suddenly you're on your way to Troy.

Later, you smell hyacinths as you fall asleep.

Glaucous

On the way to Albuquerque we saw a sign
that said ←COINS / (*something*)→ and we laughed
but now in Vermont I can't remember what *something* was.
So I go on Google Maps. I drop the little consenting
yellow person down on the highway and ask them
to look around with me. It's a fool's errand
(not the yellow they/them, they're just doing their job).

We pass ALOHA RV, and a Sheriff's car unable
to pull us over, a cyclist risking the state highway,
and all that dusty silvery grey-green sage.
There's a botanical word for that,
but I can't remember it, so I open a new tab.
I end up in an article about olive trees
written by an Italian botanist in 1993.

Then I'm in a list of botanical terms.
Aculeate, smaragdine, esquamulose
("*not* covered in scales or scale-like objects;
having a smooth skin or outer covering").
Then I ask Peri, who says "the botanical words
describe the physical characteristics that create the color."
It's too early in the day for that.

Finally Google just starts throwing words at me,
hoping one will stick: pluviosity, shalloon, tricenarian,
eudaemonic ("living life with a sense of direction").
Google is just trolling me now. I still haven't found
the word for that unearthly verdigris
that nearly made me sob with beauty
when we drove down from Denver.

So I flip back to my yellow friend and toodle down
the road a ways searching for the easy laugh, before I realize
we've gone the wrong way for miles and miles and miles.

Storm

I hear you texting me,
the phone ding from the kitchen,
but I sit still on the back stoop
with sweet coffee and the dog.

Flowers nod, bees ping back and forth.
Birds give each other advice
as a wind starts up: a tropical
storm is moving in, carrying
anything possible and wild.

I'd come in and listen to your needs
but the dog is leaning on me.
His heart beats fast against my leg,
his nose searches the air.

I'm divining the wind
with my own nose, my own heart,
feeling the clutch of excitement
as trees sway over my tight little house.

Trash Night

All those years I ignored Orion's whispers.
He hung over the garage, belt draped
sexy at his hips, asking me
you aren't really happy, are you?
I stopped up my ears.
I used tricks to keep from resenting it,
the extra work, the foul smell.
I imagined sipping a Dipper-full
of butternut squash soup,
your mother's recipe.
I hid under the giant willow
drifting its hippy arms
across the driveway,
brushing away discontent.
Every week, Sunday night,
I began again (*You're not happy*),
again the soup, the tree, those hips.
But Orion also carried a sword
I finally borrowed, when a bag broke open
and I couldn't look away anymore.

Coming Back

Some days on the path
you feel how the weight
of your ribs and your old
breasts hangs on frayed
rope safety-pinned
to your aching shoulders.

Some days the pine trees
rub complaint against each other.
You feel the bowl
of your pelvis slop
with the vast soup
of your guts, while your
hips grind in their sockets
like a ball point pen
in a dusty drawer.

Some days your head echoes
with phantom memory
or true, and the muscles
in your neck feel inadequate
to the container of your skull.

But Pileated Woodpeckers insist.
Bobcats, porcupines, weasels
impel you from the shadows.
Trees talk to each other
about the rain, and days
come when your back
feels straight and strong,
and the pine needles love
your sure and steady feet.

An America

Give me an America of picnic tables, ice cream,
jimmies and chocolate dip.
Give me an America of students
gone home for summer, locals strolling
quietly as evening cools off,
the pavement still sun-warm, ticking.

Give me an America of migrant farm workers
picking cucumbers and falling
in love, chatting at the next table
about sublets and beer. Pay them
what they've earned for welted hands,
sunburned necks, faces traced with soil-lines.

Make my America light up like neon
on a Sunday night in August
when the sound of engines dies down
and the Miss Flo diner closes up.

Put in your last order. Make it a large.
Tip the server for her patience,
for her far-away home, for her tired,
sticky, American beauty.

Hair

When my hair comes back,
it will be silver-grey and black,
curly and straight,
the hair of a witch,
a madwoman, an artist.
It will be unruly.
It will float out behind me,
grab songbirds from the air
and squeeze them till they
give up their songs.
My hair will have its own agenda.
I'll wrap my hair around
my breasts and belly
like a prayer shawl for a mad god.
My prayer will be *fuck you.*
But my hair will keep its own counsel.
It will dig its way into the earth,
between my toes tickling,
to commune with the worms.
My hair will visit with the dead
and bring back their stories.
It will teach me the slang they
use to mock the living.
My hair will know things,
and it will have no truck with anyone.
It will send out a tendril to brush
the cheeks of pretty men and women,
who will feel jittery and drunk
like two espressos and four shots of tequila.
Finally my hair will remind me
that a woman of my stature
should wear the clouds as a hat
and stride up the hills
with strong long legs
and round hips in full swing.

55-Inch Screen

I'm 51 and brand new,
and old as fuck.
I bought this huge TV
so I can watch
terrifying monsters
and technicolor heroes
grind each other down.

The tv gives me rote
old dances made bright
by the expansive digital realness
of my internet-ready splurge.

I watch it for a month
as if it might run out,
I eat candy, smoke dope,
take off my bra.
I have my own apartment,
I do whatever I want.

But then painfully
I grow up all over again.
The heroes are too young
to be interesting,
and the monsters look silly
compared to cancer,
divorce, madness.

And then the stupid big thing
sits and waits while I make bigger,
more elemental mistakes.

In a Valley

people know their skies
with an intimacy nearly lewd.
Safety-pinned to the mountains
they settle down over us
like a blanket fort—
they reach down, caress us,
go along with us.
Clouds descend daily
to stroke our cheeks,
rest like a mantle
on our shoulders.
More than a subtle flirtation,
this is love, the love of the lid
for the jar, the vault
for the money, the skin
for the bones. Does it change us?
On the Great Plains
the sky performs the arc
of parallelism, extending
endlessly in line with the earth
but infinitely never touching—
an austere and loveless bond.
But here in my valley
I lie down with cumulus,
I keep it company,
I let it consume me.

Fly

Every word the critics wrote
about that bubble-gum
spun-sugar summer song is true:
the lead singer is all ego,
and the song pure drivel,
a fantasy for fools.
I knew this.

But I jammed to it on my car radio
with the windows open anyway,
and one day at a stoplight
beautiful Latino boys seat-danced
in the next car, half my age
and twice as cool,
singing the lyrics with me.

They waved their wings
out the windows,
and their rich deep voices
flew up the suburban avenues.
I turned up my radio,
they turned up theirs;
we made peace signs
at each other and laughed.

We sang together
I just want to fly,
and it was like I wasn't
a 30-something mom
with a baby at home,
a career on hold,
and for a minute in 1999
it was summer all around me forever.

Being Alive Feels Good Again Sometimes

—for Susie Chang

Coming back from the concert
the headlights take over—
golden Klimt trees line up,
cloud-gilt chalices.

We take the same breath.

My lights throw trees,
music still shaping my mind.

A coyote crosses ahead.

His paws hit the pavement
in time to the beat in my head,
the road, the trees, my inner ear
turning, turn signal ticking
all in time and you

beside me laughing, you
beside me, my oracle.

I Saw Something in the Mirror

It's almost midnight
and I've already failed
to believe in you.

You're going to have to prove
you're really a ghost,
not some tipsy suspicion.

I'm sorry I'm not better at this.
I've only just started to watch slashers
now, in my menopausal bloom.

If I had sage, maybe, or instincts.
Let's give it some time, and some night
we might scare me to death.

Skinny-Dipping

Slippery Dip,
that subtle spring,
it froze my toes
while the sun put
its fingers in my hair.

My friend took me
and stripped down
to her cool white skin.
I tried not to see how
she glowed in the summer sun.

People swam and picked
along the bank, some beautiful,
some pimpled, full-chested,
broad-hipped, all the kinds
of bodies, frightened and new.

And finally inevitably
a perfect young man fearless
on a rock across the stream.
My eye pulled down
the dark path of his body
to his toes, curled like a child's
on the lip of the rock.

Life is unending glory.

I turned my sight inward,
thought only of the sun,
the water, that frightening rush,
and I stepped out of my skirt.

Summer Fling

Summer crashes in one day, drunk as usual
full of crude jokes and maudlin love poems,

and you can't help yourself. He's a drug, he's a bad boy,
he serves a heady cocktail of nights at 17, driving alone

past fields of fireflies, the constellations
that held your hand through heartbreak, through

the creak and snap of growing up. Summer
keeps those stars in his pocket, and brings

them out just as you tire of humidity and air conditioning,
the boring beauty of peonies, zinnias, asters.

You are seduced again, your old body feels silvery
and touchable, and before long you're drinking wine
naked by the edge of a pond, planning your next good life.

Pandemic Baking

I make the bagels on our third date,
our third Covid date, standing
in your kitchen as if we live together,
as if people aren't dying,
we aren't risking our lives.
I open a new bag of flour,
and feel it silky between my fingers
while I plouf it out over your countertop.

Flour, yeast, water, salt,
coconut sugar I brought from my pantry
because sugar isn't your thing.
Its nutty tang raises your eyebrows.
You say *this is lovely.* I can tell
you mean both the sugar and me.

The dough is tougher
than usual. I fret while it rises
but when I twirl the tori
around my finger
they feel just the right balance
of resistance and forgiveness.
The rounds go safe to the boil.

The next morning we eat them
with cream cheese, shallots,
smoked mackerel you ordered
for this purpose, thinking ahead,
thinking me lovely.
Outside your house the woods
hold close around us,
and we pretend we are safe.

Spider

I met your bathroom spider this morning.
She is lovely, slender, so delicate.
Her thorax glints iridescently.

I was hoping for inside dirt.
Our relationship is new, I don't know
all your habits as she must.

How do you hold your face
when you shave? How often do you
look in the mirror and worry?

Have you ever sat on the bathroom floor
in the middle of the night
with your head in your hands?

It would be good to know these things.
But she's no help: she gives me fables
about ropes of water and the song the drain sings,

the sound of ceramic to her infinitely
small foot. She whispers about the shift
in the air when a fly enters the room.

Her voice sooths, deliberate.
She has seen so much, but nothing
to speak of; she knows you intimately

and hardly at all. She knows
the casual cruelty of sponge and shoe,
and the sweet kindness of being overlooked.

Pumice Mines

The day we drove to the desert we had breakfast early
and nothing after—not water, not food,
only the still dry desert air.

The Sierras crouched either near or far,
no markers to reveal their size. I was bleeding,
I was a woman, ashamed in the company of two men.

I was too much in myself
in that dry place, and hoped
it was nothing worth sharing.

We drove to the pumice mines, great quiet holes
scooped in stone, work abandoned to snakes and spiders,
creatures that can wait for a mouthful of water.

I was full of love, and empty of everything.
I sat down alone on the cool floor of a mine-hole
where the white walls were too white.

The quiet carved out my belly.
When I stood up my sandal caught a burr,
and the pain was a slap. It was too much, to be a woman

in that sterile place, to be on the cusp of a life
held up in silhouette on the white walls. As we drove out
I cried for the limits of my body and my life,

and a coyote watched us go, watched us go.

About the Author

Sara Eddy is the author of two chapbooks of poetry, *Tell the Bees* (A3 Press, 2019) and *Full Mouth* (Finishing Line, 2020). She has published widely in print and online literary journals: her poems have appeared in *Threepenny Review, Baltimore Review, Raleigh Review, 2River Review,* and *Sky Island Journal,* among other venues. She holds a Ph.D. in American Literature from Tufts University and works as Assistant Director of the Jacobson Center for Writing at Smith College, in Northampton, Massachusetts. She is mother to two remarkable human beings, and lives in Amherst, Massachusetts, in a house built by Emily Dickinson's cousin.

§

www.ingramcontent.com/pod-product-compliance
Lightning Source LLC
Chambersburg PA
CBHW071332190426
43193CB00041B/1754